Fundamentals of Evaluating Sign Language Programs

Checklists for Program Assessment

by Mike Kemp, Ed.D.

DawnSignPress

San Diego, California

10 9 8 7 6 5 4 3 2 1

ATTENTION

Quantity discounts for organizations, schools, bookstores, and
distributors are available.

For information, please contact:

DawnSignPress
6130 Nancy Ridge Drive
San Diego, CA 92121
619-625-0600 V/TTY   619-625-2336 FAX
ORDER TOLL FREE 1-800-549-5350
www.dawnsign.com

Table of Contents

This book is dedicated to my son, Bill Kemp.

Acknowledgements

M Y FIRST THANKS go to Dr. Jimmy Fortune, a professor of Educational Research at the Virginia Polytechnic Institute and State University, who served as a catalyst in getting this book started in 1981 when I was a doctoral student. My sincere thanks also go to DawnSignPress, Joe Dannis, and his production staff who helped make *Fundamentals of Evaluating Sign Language Programs* a better book. My genuine appreciation and thanks are extended to Roger C. Carver, my best and closest friend and confidant, for filling up my manuscript's first draft with red pen marks asking for clarification on many issues. My deep thanks go to Dr. Judy Johnson and Lynn Jacobowitz, my long-time colleagues at Gallaudet University for their time in reviewing the manuscript. My heartfelt appreciation and thanks go to my family members, my son Bill, Jamie, Jennifer and their mother, for the encouragement, and for letting me hole up in the loft at home where I wrote the book. Above all, thank you Joan for giving me all the support, love, and understanding I needed while writing this book. You are a dear!

Introduction

THE Fundamentals of Evaluating Sign Language Programs is designed to be a guide in evaluating sign language programs in the United States and in any country where people have an interest in learning a signed language. While the book's main focus is on American Sign Language (ASL) programs, its basic principles of evaluation can be applied to any sign language program.

American Sign Language programs are growing in number. There are more than 2,000 ASL programs in the United States. Beyond church- and community-organized ASL classes, colleges, universities, federal, state, and local governments, non-profit organizations as well as public and private schools also offer ASL classes. In Sheryl Cooper's dissertation "Academic Status of Sign Language Programs in Institutions of Higher Education in the United States," she states that sign language is an emerging academic discipline (Cooper, 1997). Underscoring Cooper's assertion, ASL's growth and popularity are evidenced in Sherman Wilcox's Internet home page. The page provides information regarding American Sign Language as a foreign language as well as a list of colleges and universities that accept American Sign Language classes for their students' foreign language requirements. For additional information on the Internet, go to:

http://www.unm.edu/~wilcox/ASLFL/univlist.html

Although ASL is becoming more widespread, existing sign language programs continue to have different goals and objectives along with different notions of how programs should be run to meet these goals and objectives. ASL training for teachers and program directors has always emphasized teaching methodology, curriculum development, and student progress evaluation. In spite of this emphasis, very little literature, if any, has been written about evaluating such training or the resulting programs. The information in this book is an expansion of my article published in the American Annals of the Deaf (Kemp, 1988). The main purpose of this publication is to assist a program director/coordinator in assessing an ASL program, and to determine whether there is a need for adjustments or additions to a program.

This book is divided into three parts. Part One offers a brief background of the evaluation process. Part Two provides explanations of program evaluation questions. Eight areas will be examined: Personnel selection, curriculum, placement interviews, media utilization, teachers' performance, environmental aspects, supervisory effectiveness, and budget. Part Three contains appendices which offer sample evaluation forms for program directors/coordinators to use while assessing their ASL programs.

At the time this book was written, there were no established standards for an ASL program to follow in order to be considered an effective program. It is possible that this book will serve as a catalyst for establishing such standards as determined by an accreditation organization. It must be emphasized here that this book is only a guide to determining whether the program has resources in place that will facilitate an effective delivery system. The delivery system's outcome would be, of course, to produce students whose sign language skills are sufficient enough to communicate with members of the Deaf community. In no way should this book be used to determine whether a program has met acceptable standards. As ASL grows and becomes more standardized, evaluation will also become more sophisticated and refined. The information here is intended to inform, but is also intended to start a dialog. At the back of this book, you will find a questionnaire designed to gather information for a second edition. As the people who shape ASL instruction now and in the future, I hope you take the time to fill out and return this survey. With this type of collaborative effort, we can move ahead together and improve the ability to evaluate sign language programs.

Part One

Purpose of Evaluating Sign Language Programs

W HY SHOULD WE EVALUATE American Sign Language programs? This question deserves an answer. Historically, professional American Sign Language (ASL) instructors focused on the various methods of teaching sign language and evaluating their students' skills. This emphasis on methodology and students' progress should always remain. Yet one tool is lacking; an evaluation method that would ensure quality programs and further instructors' abilities to focus on student progress. There is a scarcity of literature geared toward monitoring the quality and effectiveness of sign language programs and also limited literature on evaluating foreign and second language programs (Lynch, 1996; Alderson & Beretta Eds., 1992). So, although there are a few general guides to language programs, none is specifically for ASL. ASL is a distinct and genuine language; it makes sense that ASL programs have evaluative mechanisms designed for their needs.

In Sanders' *Evaluating School Programs: An Educator's Guide* (1992), the author states that evaluation can help with the development of a successful program. Evaluation can help the program directors and/or coordinator determine the degree of their program's success. Stufflebeam and colleagues (1975) define the reason for evaluation:

> The main purpose of an evaluation is not to prove but to improve.

True! We need to use evaluation as a tool to see how completely we have achieved our program's goals. If we do not evaluate, then how do we know we are accomplishing our goals?

Tuckman reinforces this point by stating that the purpose of "evaluating an instructional program is to provide the means for determining whether the program is meeting its goals; that is, whether the measured outcomes for a given set of instructional inputs match the intended or pre-specified outcomes" (1979). He further wrote:

> The sole purpose of evaluating an instructional program is to determine how "on-target" it is by comparing achieved outcomes with intended ones.

This book will not attempt to guide program coordinators/directors in developing their goals and objectives; those should be specific to each program. Rather, this book will help evaluate how well a program is succeeding, keeping in mind the unique features of ASL. Sign language programs are unique in the sense that the target language is visually oriented. When comparing ASL with other foreign language educational programs, one must remember the distinct features of this visually oriented environment. These features include video equipment, correct classroom lighting, classroom seating arrangements, and so on. This book considers these features while providing information on evaluating a program.

2

Background

Public school systems became widespread by the 1920s, and educators realized a need for a rigid system that would allow pupils to proceed from one level to the next in an orderly fashion. Specifically, this required the development of standardized ability and achievement tests, and resulted in the rapid creation of new evaluation designs, approaches, and instruments to measure pupil progress. During the next thirty years, evaluation accelerated, assessing student performance based on experimentation with new content, new methods and new materials. Ralph W. Tyler (1942), in his eight-year-study of the 1930s, asserted that educators should carefully define their objectives and collect the data needed to determine whether they had been achieved.

In an attempt to improve educational opportunities for minorities, the disadvantaged, and the handicapped, the United States Congress passed the Elementary and Secondary Education Act for Children in 1965. This act gave school districts across the nation the chance to seek federal funds for new programs in mathematics, science, and foreign languages. In return, the law mandated that recipients evaluate their own programs and report to their sponsors (Schaffarzick & Sykes, 1979). This requirement triggered the expansion of evaluation of educational programs and student progress (Popham, 1975).

There are now a great number of publications available related to evaluating programs. The Washington (Washington, DC) Resource Library Center contains many entries on program evaluations covering the basic educational areas. The very number of such publications is a clear indication that the field of educational program

3

evaluation is expanding. Evaluating sign language programs can be considered a new addition to the growing list of specialized program evaluations.

Who Should Be Evaluators?

Although it is not always possible, it is recommended that an outside evaluator conduct a program evaluation (Popham, 1975; Morris & Fitz-Gibbon, 1978; Fitz-Gibbon & Morris, 1987; Isaac & Michael, 1983; Windham & Chapman, 1990). It is difficult to maintain objectivity while evaluating one's own program, and the credibility of an internal evaluation could be questioned and scrutinized by skeptics. Although programs have limited ability to evaluate themselves, limited by anything from funding to size of the program, these limitations should not discourage programs from self-evaluation. Some evaluation is better than no evaluation.

The evaluator should be knowledgeable not only in the area of teaching American Sign Language, but also in the area of program evaluation. A person with at least ten years of teaching experience and five years of administrative experience would qualify as an expert.

When Should Evaluation Take Place?

Evaluation can happen at different times during the planning and conducting of a program. Windham and Chapman (1990) suggest that evaluation take place:

Prior to the program's implementation. This can serve as a needs assessment time to assist the program director/coordinator by justifying the purchase of equipment or hiring additional personnel.

4

During the program's implementation (formative). On-going evaluation can be useful. Periodic evaluations, while being a tool for needs assessment in regard to equipment purchases or personnel additions, can also provide justification for continuing a program.

At the end of a program/project (summative). As is the case with the first two evaluation times, this can be a time to justify equipment purchases or personnel additions.

The time required to complete the evaluation depends on the type of evaluation and on when the evaluation takes place. Evaluations prior to and at the end of a program may only require a day or two. Formative evaluations done throughout the program's implementation can happen as frequently as the program director/coordinator feels is necessary.

All personnel and students should be informed when evaluations are taking place so that all involved can participate to the best of their abilities, making the evaluation process more valuable for everyone.

What Should Be Done Afterward?

Once the evaluation has been completed, the program director/coordinator can assess the program's needs. Needs assessment is used to improve the program's delivery system as well as its effectiveness. Decisions to make major purchases such as video equipment or new desks can be the result of a needs assessment.

No program is perfect. By looking for room to improve, a program can optimize its features and make them more effective.

Part Two
Program Assessment

This book should be used as a guide to evaluation. This book does not promote one set of goals and objectives, but rather, presents information about evaluation with the understanding that program directors/coordinators have already developed program-specific goals and objectives that reflect the program's approach to teaching ASL. The personnel within a given program may want to review the contents of this book and determine whether the program should undergo an informal assessment, a full-fledged program evaluation by outsiders, or both. Regardless of the type of evaluation, the program needs to determine whether its goals and objectives could be improved, changed, or found in part to be obsolete. Remembering that evaluation is not to prove but to improve, the following eight areas should be assessed:

Personnel selection
Curriculum
Placement interview

Media utilization
Teachers' performance evaluation
Environmental aspects of a classroom
Supervisor's effectiveness
Budget

Each of the eight areas has a checklist with evaluative questions. In this section each checklist question is given with an explanation. For easy use and reference, the checklists are repeated in the back of the book without the explanations. A person doing an informal assessment should conduct the evaluation with an open mind. Objectivity must be maintained. Once the informal assessment is done, then the planning and implementation process can begin for the formal evaluation by outsiders.

Personnel Selection Checklist

This checklist will assist the program directors/coordinators in determining the thoroughness of hiring procedures. Depending on the size and scope of the program, not all of the questions listed below may be relevant.

1. Does the program advertise to recruit prospective ASL teachers in various publications such as Deaf Life, NAD Broadcaster, Deaf Nation, Sign Language Studies, Journal of Deaf Studies and Deaf Education, Deaf Studies, American Annals of the Deaf, Silent News, American Sign Language Teachers Association Newsletter, and Chronicles of Higher Education?

Advertising job openings is essential for a program to attract qualified ASL teachers. The demand for skilled ASL teachers is high in competitive markets, and programs have to compete with each other for the best teachers. The publications

8

mentioned are distributed on the national level and the audience is widespread. In no way does this list exhaust all avenues of advertisement, but it does highlight basic publications that prospective ASL teachers would be likely to seek out. Addresses and phone numbers of these publications can be found in Appendix A.

2. Does the program conduct national searches for prospective ASL teachers?

In an effort to attract the most highly qualified teachers, national hiring searches may be required. The definition of a "highly qualified" teacher is one who possesses excellent ASL skills, has been awarded certification by the American Sign Language Teachers Association, and is certified by the state's department of education (if applicable). A broadened search can be achieved by submitting job announcements to the publications listed in Appendix A.

3. Does the program provide a clear and concise job description for the position being advertised?

Candidates looking for a teaching position need to know if the job being advertised is full time, part time, seasonal, contract, course-by-course, permanent or temporary, and when the job begins. Salary range should be noted along with benefits such as health and life insurance. In addition, a list of duties should be spelled out. See Sample Job Description on page 10.

4. Does the program require prospective ASL teachers to provide professional references?

A minimum of three references is recommended. Such references can be important, especially if they come from Deaf adults who recognize the instructor as a bona fide user of ASL who respects the language and Deaf Culture.

Sample Job Description

CLERC UNIVERSITY ANNOUNCES
A FACULTY POSITION VACANCY

The Department of American Sign Language in the Clerc University School of Professional Studies announces a faculty position at the Instructor or Assistant Professor level, Ph.D. preferred. The position is primarily in the area of teaching ASL. Responsibilities include:

- Teach both graduate and undergraduate ASL courses
- Participate in development and revision of curricula for both new and existing programs
- Assume normal faculty responsibilities as assigned.

Qualifications:

- Ph.D. preferred in Deaf Studies, ASL Studies, Applied Linguistics, ASL Linguistics, or Second Language Acquisition/Teaching. Candidates without a Ph.D. will be considered based on their experience within the field of teaching ASL.
- Five years of experience teaching ASL in a formal program; prior experience in another relevant area (e.g., Interpreting, ASL Literature, Deaf Culture, etc.) is also considered helpful.
- ASLTA Professional certification highly preferred.

Salary and Rank:

Commensurate with education and related experience.

Deadline for Application: December 1, 1999

Position Available: August 16, 2000

Send letter of application and resume to:

Dr. John H. Williams
ASL Search Committee
Department of ASL
Clerc University
Neffsville, KA (fictional)

Clerc University is an Equal Opportunity Employer/Educational Institution

10

5. Is there a screening/interviewing committee in the program to review applications?

This question may be more relevant for programs at the college or university level. The screening/interviewing committee should consist of the program director or coordinator and two or three ASL teachers from the program, preferably members of the Deaf community. One outsider may join the committee, if desired, to provide a perspective from outside of the program. The purpose of setting up a committee like this is to ensure that objectivity is maintained. A screening/interviewing committee is strongly recommended. If there are none, then the person who makes the hiring decisions becomes highly vulnerable to criticism.

6. Does the screening/interviewing committee have established criteria for selecting prospective ASL teachers?

The criteria that the committee spells out will speed up the process of selecting teachers. Criteria also protect the committee members from charges of favoritism, nepotism, or "returning favors" in their selection process.

7. Do the criteria, mentioned in number 6, include, but not limit themselves to, the following?

A. Does the applicant have the required minimum number of years of experience teaching ASL?

A minimum three years of teaching experience is suggested. Novice teachers may require two to three years before they build up professional self-confidence and a familiarity with the methods of teaching, curriculum, and evaluation. If the program is hiring teachers for a specific population such as K–12 or adults, finding candidates with direct experience with that specific population is beneficial. More than any other qualification, it is essential that the teacher be fluent in the use of ASL, and it is strongly preferable that the applicant has not only recently completed ASL classes.

Recent literature (Jacobs, 1996) suggests that American Sign Language is a very unique language when compared with other commonly learned languages and that it may take 2,400 to 2,760 hours of instruction for a person to attain a mid-level proficiency (Walker, 1989, cited in Jacobs, 1996). Even at that proficiency level an applicant's ability to teach ASL is an important consideration.

B. Does the applicant hold the minimum degree requirement in his/her field or in related field(s)?

Several colleges and universities offer a Bachelor of Arts degree in teaching ASL. There are a small number of programs that offer a Masters degree in teaching ASL. Other fields that may be related are Deaf Studies, ASL Studies, Applied Linguistics, ASL Linguistics, Second Language Acquisition/Teaching, or Education (not only Deaf Education). Degrees in these related fields along with ASL fluency and experience may qualify applicants to teach ASL.

C. Does the applicant possess teaching credentials?

A number of states require teachers in public schools or community colleges to possess teaching credentials. Program directors need to check their school's policy and their state's department of education about credential requirements. Some schools require a review of applicants' credentials prior to hiring.

D. Does the applicant hold a certificate awarded by the American Sign Language Teachers Association (ASLTA) under the auspices of the National Association of the Deaf? If yes, which certificate—Provisional, Qualified or Professional?

Candidates receive the Provisional certificate after satisfying the minimum requirements as detailed by ASLTA. The requirements for receiving the Qualified and the Professional certificates are rigorous. The candidate must pass an examination and appear before an interviewing committee before being awarded the Professional level certification. The Provisional certification is valid for four years and can be extended an additional four years by special request. The Qualified and Professional level certifications are valid for eight years and are renewable after meeting requirements spelled out by the Evaluation Committee under the auspices of the American Sign Language Teachers Association. If a state Board of Education certification is not required, ASLTA certification at any of the three levels is recommended to ensure the quality of the program.

E. Did the applicant attend various conferences and/or workshops pertaining to ASL teaching or any related fields?

If the person has attended ASL Linguistics, ASLTA, Deaf Researchers, ASL Literature, or Deaf Studies conferences, this indicates that the candidate keeps up with the trends and issues related to ASL teaching. The person would likely have current information about the newest methods for teaching and evaluating ASL students. There are constant opportunities for exposure to new developments and new research findings related to ASL and teaching as well as to technological advancements that may benefit ASL programs. To get information about various workshops for ASL teachers go to the ASLTA home page at

http://www.isc.rit.edu/~ASLTAwww/

F. Can the applicant use various types of media and technology for teaching ASL?

The ability to use media in the classroom is essential to a successful teaching career in ASL. ASL is a visual–gestural language, making the use of video equipment and other visual media for instructional purposes quite extensive.

G. Is the applicant aware of the various approaches and methods of teaching a second language?

This inquiry can be made during the interview. The candidate should be able to identify the various methods and approaches of teaching a second language. Familiarity with methods and terminology is a good indication of the candidate's skills related to second language teaching.

H. Does the applicant demonstrate acceptance for diversity among people, especially toward hearing people who want to learn ASL?

Acceptance may be difficult for the candidate to demonstrate conclusively in an interview setting. It is imperative, however, that the applicant have a positive attitude toward all students. The interviewer may want to ask questions such as "Are you willing to have a class with students from different ethnic backgrounds?" or "What would you do if a student makes a racial slur in your classroom?" By making the candidate aware of the programs, policies on tolerance and diversity during the interview, the program can avoid problems down the road.

I. Is the applicant fluent in the use of American Sign Language?

A candidate's ASL skills cannot be determined by observation alone. A Language Proficiency Interview (LPI) is a tool that is used by the U.S. State Department to assess the foreign language skills of its personnel before assigning them overseas. Two evaluation tools, Sign Communication Proficiency Interview (SCPI) and American Sign Language Proficiency Interview (ASLPI), were adapted from LPI and are used to assess either sign communication or ASL skills. ASLPI is recommended to determine the candidate's skills. A rating of 4 or 4+ (Advanced or Advanced Plus) is considered fluent but not Native (rating of 5). Keep in mind that the person administering the ASLPI must have a proficiency level of 5. Training is furnished to individuals who are interested in becoming an ASLPI interviewer, rater, or both.

J. Does the applicant show the ability to develop detailed lesson plans?

A detailed lesson plan consists of many things, including clearly written behavioral objectives, task analyses, and expected outcomes. A lesson plan should be written in such a way that a substitute teacher would be able to follow the plan without much difficulty. The lesson plan should include pre-learning activities, learning activities, use of media, objectives, and assignments. The applicant should be asked to furnish a lesson plan portfolio at the time of the interview.

K. Does the applicant give a satisfactory answer on how a student with special learning needs is to be handled?

This question refers to students with special-needs issues such as learning disabilities, arthritis, visual impairment, cerebral palsy, or advanced age. An example of such a question is "How would you handle a student with vision impairment in your class?"

L. Does the applicant have training in developing relevant tests?

A teacher should have some training in giving tests to students in class. It is important to keep in mind that the tests are based on what was covered in class and not what will be covered in the future.

M. Is the applicant knowledgeable about the Acculturation Model related to successful second language acquisition?

Acculturation Model provides information pertaining to what enables students to master target languages. See Gingras' *Second Language Acquisition and Foreign Language*

Teaching for further information. Also see Schumann's *Research on the Acculturation Model for Second Language Acquisition* as well as Kemp's "An Acculturation Model for Learners of American Sign Language" in Lucas' *Sociolinguistics in Deaf Community Series*, Volume 4 (1998).

N. Is the applicant knowledgeable about Deaf Culture?

When teaching a language, culture is to be included in the lesson plans. Language and culture depend on each other in order to evolve. There are cultural behaviors such as attention-getting, acknowledging, confirming, taboos, etc., of which ASL students must be made aware while learning the target language. The teacher must demonstrate competence in this area. The applicant should be able to answer questions about Deaf Culture and exhibit familiarity with current literature related to Deaf Culture.

O. Is the applicant capable of including cultural information in lesson plans?

The candidate may be knowledgeable about Deaf Culture, but can s/he apply the information through the lesson plans? Such information needs to be evaluated while reviewing the lesson plan portfolio. For example, a teacher would include the ways of getting a person's attention when initiating conversation.

8. Did the screening/interviewing committee develop a personnel selection form to assist with the decision making process and selection of the final candidates for the job?

Appendix C is a personnel selection form. The personnel committee members may feel free to make changes to the form to accommodate their program's needs. It is recommended, however, that the standards reflected in the appendix not be compromised.

9. Did the interview committee develop a list of questions, organized so each member can take a turn asking questions of the applicant?

A list of suggested interview questions can be found in Appendix D.

Curriculum Checklist

A sound curriculum consists of goals and objectives, and the use of clear behavioral terms, in addition to textbooks and teaching materials. Literature is available on curriculum and instructional development. Check with a local professional library for additional information. A program's curriculum is developed by a content specialist and a curriculum specialist. A content specialist is a person who has expertise in teaching ASL and who possesses knowledge about the linguistics of ASL. A curriculum specialist, using the information supplied by the content specialist, develops the curriculum. Hiring one person as both content and curriculum specialist is not recommended. Such a person would be so involved with the dual responsibilities of these jobs that they might not be able to evaluate the curriculum globally.

If the program has a curriculum, then respond to the following questions shown in Appendix E:

1. Was the curriculum developed through the efforts of content specialists along with a curriculum specialist?

An ideal situation is to have a content specialist and a curriculum specialist work as a team to develop a curriculum.

The content expert should be knowledgeable about second language teaching, ASL linguistics, and Deaf Culture. The curriculum specialist, with help from the content specialist, would write specific items such as goals, behavioral objectives, and task analyses, as well as tests. To save costs, a program may want to use one of its veteran sign language teachers as its content specialist. A curriculum specialist could be found in the Department of Education of a local college to collaborate with the content specialist and develop the program's curriculum.

2. Does the curriculum include the program's general goals related to student achievement levels?

The curriculum should spell out the goals and purposes of a given program. Is the program's intention to produce students with a high level of signing skills? Or, to produce interpreters? Each program has its own reasons for offering sign language classes, such as to train prospective teachers and counselors of the Deaf. The purpose of a program can make a difference in its approach to teaching sign language. For example, the approach to teaching sign language in K–12 classes is different from that of teaching adults. Approaches toward teaching ASL as a foreign language where foreign language requirements are applicable would be different from those used in teaching ASL as a second language. For information about acceptance of ASL as a foreign language go to this home page:

http://www.unm.edu/~wilcox/ASLFL/asl_fl.html.

3. Does the curriculum list specific performance objectives for each course?

Specific performance objectives should be spelled out in each course's syllabus. Objectives should be written in such a manner that teachers know the behavior students must exhibit to attain the program's general goals. See Mager's *Preparing Instructional Objectives* (Revised 2nd Edition).

4. Are behavioral terms used in the performance objectives?

A list of behavioral terms can be found in Mager's *Preparing Instructional Objectives* (Revised 2nd Edition). The list includes terms such as *to write, to identify, to compare, to list*. These terms are concise, to the point, and measurable. Other more vague terms such as *understand, appreciate,* and *explain* are too broad and cannot be measured.

5. Is the curriculum subject to periodic revisions?

On-going linguistic and second language research findings will make a difference in how future sign language classes are taught. An annual review for possible revisions is recommended. The program director/coordinator and the teachers should meet to discuss possible changes in the curriculum.

6. Is flexibility allowed for last-minute changes in the curriculum if a teacher sees fit?

There may be times when a teacher feels that the contents of the curriculum are inappropriate for a variety of reasons. The teacher should be able to make minor revisions when appropriate.

7. Is the teacher expected to inform others of any last-minute changes in the curriculum?

Communication between teachers and the program director/coordinator is a must—a fact that cannot be stressed enough. Consistency in a program is a strong indication that the professional staff are working together as a team.

8. If a teacher does make changes to the curriculum and informs the director/coordinator, are other teachers informed of these changes in the curriculum?

This question underscores the importance of open communication between the teachers and the program director/coordinator. If the teachers are not made aware of changes, then the quality control of the curriculum and the program itself can be affected.

9. Is the curriculum made readily available for teachers to review?

The teachers will have a sense of ownership if given the opportunity to review the curriculum or any changes to the curriculum. Access to this information can provide solidarity among the staff members.

10. Is a word processor available for the staff members to write up or make changes in the curriculum?

With the aid of a word processor, the curriculum can be quickly and easily revised without extensive retyping.

11. Are syllabi distributed to the students on the first day of class?

The students need to know the teacher's expectations throughout the semester or quarter. A syllabus is considered a contract between the teacher and the students. If a student does not like what the teacher expects of him or her, he or she is at liberty to drop the class before the second meeting of the class. Syllabi can serve to protect both the teacher and the student in case of disputes. The syllabus consists of the following: course description, performance objectives, course requirements, performance evaluation, grading system, and the teacher's office location and office hours. Here is a sample syllabus for an ASL I course.

SAMPLE SYLLABUS

Department: American Sign Language
Title: ASL 101—American Sign Language I
Credit Hours: 3
Instructor: Dr. Mike Kemp
Internet: mike.kemp@gallaudet.edu
TTY: 202-651-5286
Office: Dawes House
Hours: M-F 2:00–3:30 pm.

Course Description: This course will provide students with the basic skills and knowledge of American Sign Language. It will introduce targeted lexical items through readiness activities by means of structured and conversational approaches. Students will be exposed to commands, questions, and statements in ASL. Regulating behaviors, such as attention-getting devices and turn taking, will be introduced and demonstrated both receptively and expressively by students. Additional lexical items will be acquired under the grammatical topics of sentence types, time, and pronominalization.

Performance Objectives: The student will:
- Produce ASL sentences to ask for and give names;
- Produce ASL sentences to exchange personal information;
- Produce ASL sentences to talk about surroundings;
- Produce ASL sentences to ask for and give basic directions;
- Produce ASL sentences to talk about the family;
- Produce ASL sentences to talk about activities;
- Produce ASL sentences to apologize, give reasons, express opinions, suggest;
- Produce ASL sentences with numbers ranging from 1 to 100;
- Produce ASL sentences with the following grammatical features:
    Yes/no questions
    Wh-questions
    Personal pronouns
    Spatial referencing
    Agent marker
    Negation
    Non-manual markers
    Possessive pronouns
    Role shifting
    Limb classifiers

Course Requirements:
- Class attendance and participation;
- Attend events (such as a Fall Play Production at a Theatre—additional information will be furnished);
- Weekly journal;
- Take quizzes; and
- Final examination.

Performance Evaluation and Grading System:
- Participation in class   10%
- Weekly journal   20%
- Quizzes   40%
- Final examination

12. Does the program have a means of evaluating its materials to determine their effectiveness?

McIntire's *Evaluating Sign Language Teaching and Learning Materials* can be used to evaluate the textbooks and the teaching materials. Apparently, there are no other published guides focusing on the effectiveness of ASL teaching materials.

13. Are the teaching materials subject to periodic change or replacement?

Due to the availability of new materials, or wear and tear on the existing materials, the program should allow for periodic change or replacement of materials. The program director/coordinator and/or the teachers can decide when to make changes. One must bear in mind the budget issues related to replacing teaching materials.

Placement Interview Checklist

A placement interview can be used to determine a student's skill level in sign language in order to assess the student's preparedness for a particular class. A placement interview is conducted in ASL, with the interviewer asking the student basic questions and evaluating the signed response for skill level. The skills evaluated can include comprehension of basic questions, ability to fingerspell, ability to give directions, and use of classifiers, among other skills. Appendix F contains a list of questions that can determine the effectiveness of a program's placement policy.

1. Does each course have a defined entrance level for determining a student's placement in the appropriate

course and a defined exit level to ensure proper advancement to the next level course?

To ensure that incoming students are properly placed and to ensure student performance at each level is appropriate, each course should have a test for entrance level.

2. Are the exit level for the previous course and the entrance level for the next course consistent?

The exit level for Level One must be the same as the entrance level for Level Two.

3. Are both the entrance and exit levels subject to periodic revisions?

As mentioned in the Curriculum Checklist section, the curriculum is subject to periodic revisions. If there are changes to the curriculum, then the program director/coordinator needs to determine whether changes in the entrance and exit levels for each level are required.

4. Are students who have taken sign language classes elsewhere required to take placement interviews to determine appropriate placement?

Classes with a disparity in skill level can make a teacher's job much more difficult. It is a good idea to require students with credit in sign language from another program to have a placement interview. Because the teaching of ASL is still relatively in its infancy, the programs throughout the United States have yet to standardize any one curriculum. A student who took ASL III in one part of the country may not be ready to take ASL II as defined by a different program. Placement interviews enable students to be placed in the appropriate class.

5. If a student successfully attains the exit level for a course, is s/he automatically eligible for entry into the next level without undergoing a placement interview?

This can be a tricky situation. The task of interviewing students after each level can be time consuming. If the program director/coordinator has confidence in the effectiveness of the entrance and exit criteria for each level, then such interviews are not necessary for the students who have taken classes within the program beginning at the first level. However, a program may have the students take the placement interview every two levels. Periodic placement tests at pre-determined levels may assure the quality of the program.

6. Are placement interviews scheduled regularly so prospective students can be interviewed prior to registration?

Regularly scheduled interviews improve chances of a student being placed properly and registering in the correct level class.

7. Are returning students required to have a placement interview after an absence of one year?

Returning students may have lost sign language skills. If the period of time between taking classes or practicing is prolonged, a placement interview is necessary.

8. When conducting a placement interview, are the following factors taken into consideration?

A. Prospective student's test anxiety?

Student anxiety can skew the results of the interview, possibly causing an inappropriate placement in class.

B. Interview room climate?

An adverse climate, such as a room with an uncomfortable temperature, can affect a student's performance, possibly causing an inappropriate placement.

C. Lighting quality in the interview room?

The lighting quality is essential for effective communication in a sign language placement interview. The interviewer and the prospective student should be seated so that they can see each other without difficulty. The light coming from a window should never be to the back of either the interviewer or the prospective student, because it can cause a silhouette effect. Adequate lighting also reduces eye fatigue, a condition which could cause miscommunication.

D. Interviewer's qualities:

Is s/he friendly?

Is s/he compassionate?

Does s/he possess excellent interpersonal skills?

The above interviewer qualities are necessary in order to make the prospective students comfortable during the placement interview. Public relations is a part of student placement, and people-oriented personnel can aid in promoting the program.

Does s/he show consistency in placement recommendations?

Does s/he know and understand the contents of the program's curriculum?

Is s/he punctual in showing up for the placement interviews?

Does s/he wear appropriate attire for the interviews?

Because sign language is a visual language, we need to minimize "visual noise." Flashy clothes with clashing colors or loud prints can be very distracting to students.

9. Are the results of the placement interviews made available to the prospective students within a reasonable amount of time?

Students need to know the placement results so that registration can take place immediately after a decision is made. Timeliness in offering placement results is one way to assure revenue. Students should be informed of when they can expect results, and results of the placement interview should be sent to the student within two days. If a student waits for an extended period of time and receives no decision from the program, s/he may register elsewhere or simply lose interest.

Media Utilization Checklist

Media utilization is mandatory for any teacher of a course in ASL. ASL is a visual–gestural language that uses visual media as a teaching tool. Appendix G is a checklist for evaluating a program's use of such media.

1. Does the program have access to the following video equipment?

VCR? TV monitor? Camcorder? Computer with CD-ROM? Laptop computer and multimedia projector?

Like the ideal lab for any spoken foreign language program, a sign language program should have the equipment mentioned above. Because sign language is a visual–gestural language, TV monitors, VCRs, and camcorders are needed to allow the students to observe their own progress. Televisions with at least 35-inch monitors are best.

2. Does the program take security precautions in maintaining video equipment?

A. Anchor pads?

Anchor pads are used to secure the video equipment while in the classroom. Thefts are prevalent in any educational program.

B. Sign-up sheets for teachers who want to use the equipment?

Sign-up sheets for use of the video equipment are recommended in order to minimize loss or damage.

C. A storage area with dead-bolt lock?

The video equipment, when not in the classroom, can be put in a storage room. A dead-bolt lock is an economical means of securing the video equipment. A hasp lock with a padlock or combination lock is not recommended as it can be easily pried off.

D. Security cables?

Security cables are used to secure camcorders that are set up to be used in conjunction with a VCR and a monitor. The cables may prove to be cumbersome, but at least the equipment is secured.

E. Identification marks on the equipment?
Such marks make it difficult for thieves to resell the equipment. Identification marks also make the recovery of stolen equipment easier.

F. Inventory information?

An inventory sheet will enable the program director/coordinator to determine if any equipment is missing.

3. Does the program have VCR head cleaners?

VCR head cleaners need to be readily available. VCR heads tend to get dirty, which results in inferior picture quality.

4. Does the program provide teachers in-service training on media utilization?

It is best to make sure that all teachers are knowledgeable about the media used in a program. Damage to equipment caused by a lack of training in proper equipment is an unnecessary and can be costly.

5. If reservations for use of video equipment from a central facility on campus are required, do teachers know where to call or go to make reservations?

If this kind of requirement is necessary for a program to insure video equipment availability, then this information must be given to teachers.

6. Do teachers know the policy for reserving and use of the video equipment?

There are places where reservations must be made two or three days in advance. If advance reservation is required and a teacher tries to secure reservations ten minutes before a class starts, this can cause a great deal of friction between the audio–visual people and the sign language program.

7. Does the program use commercially produced videocassettes or CD-ROMs for use in the classroom and/or lab?

Commercially produced videocassettes and CD-ROMs can be excellent teaching tools for classroom use. They provide talented role models for ASL students to follow. In addition, the videocassettes and CD-ROMs can complement the textbooks being used. Information on commercially produced resources can be obtained by contacting Gallaudet Bookstore, the National Association of the Deaf, or ASLTA.

8. Does a program's teachers have the opportunity to produce their own video presentations for exclusive use in the classroom?

Teacher-produced tapes can be used effectively for instructional purposes. They are more cost effective than inviting live guest speakers in the event of budget restraints. Teachers can use the videocassettes more than once over a long period of time, saving time in lesson planning.

9. Does the program have an adequate number of blank videocassettes for teachers to use?

Teachers can develop their own video presentations for use in the classroom if blank videocassettes are provided to them. A videocassette can be an important teaching tool.

10. Are the program's videocassettes and CD-ROMs labeled and organized in such a way as to provide easy access?

A good labeling and storage system can save time when dealing with visual media cassettes and disks.

11. Does the program provide various items that can be used for object manipulations in the classroom such as Lego toys, small dolls, etc.?

Object manipulations using doll houses, toy cars, and miniature dolls, can be an effective in teaching sign language (See Cokely and Baker's *ASL: A Teacher's Text on Curriculum, Methods, and Evaluation*).

12. Does the program provide teachers with funds to purchase teaching materials for their classes?

Money can be a catalyst for teacher creativity. Teacher innovations occur outside of the classroom, and if there is no money to support the development of these innovations, then teacher creativity can suffer. There is no standard amount of money required. Some programs have this kind of expense in their budget.

13. Do the teachers have access to the following items:

     A. Overhead projector and a screen?
     B. Blank transparencies?
     C. Commercially prepared transparencies?
     D. Slide projector and slide tray(s)?
     E. Chalk or water-based markers?
     F. Laptop computer and multimedia projector?
     G. Copy machine?

14. Do the teachers have access to a word processor to type up lesson plans?

Writing lesson plans is a time-consuming and at times cumbersome task. The use of a word processor for lesson plan creation allows a person to make minor revisions to an existing lesson plan without re-typing the entire page. This will save a great deal of time and leave the teacher free to be creative in developing new teaching tools.

15. Does the program have a lab for students to use?

A program with a complete lab can provide effective services to students who need to complete assignments outside of the classroom. A lab can have workstations with a VCR, a TV monitor, and possibly a camcorder. Also, the lab can have a library of ASL videocassettes. In a lab environment students have the opportunity to practice their comprehension skills by viewing tapes from the video library or by monitoring their own expressive skills via the use of a camcorder. Another possible feature in a lab is a closed-circuit system, which would allow students and teachers to interact using camcorders.

16. Does the program have a person (a student assistant) present at the lab to assist the students?

Today's lab is incomplete without a lab assistant. The risk in having students unsupervised in a lab can be great, especially when considering program liability and insurance.

17. Is there adequate lighting in the lab for camcorders?

Adequate lighting is important for students when they videotape themselves. Bad lighting can cause a difficult-to-review tape. This problem can be alleviated by camcorders whose lux requirement allows for lower lighting.

18. Does the lab have solid color backgrounds in front of which the student can stand while filming themselves with the camcorder?

Solid backgrounds provide a clearer view of the student's signing when viewing the recording on a monitor.

19. Is the lab accessible to students during non-class times?

Programs that offer evening classes need to have facilities that ensure access for both their daytime and their evening students.

20. Are there procedures for both teachers and lab assistants to report malfunctioning visual media equipment?

Repair request forms need to be available for teachers and lab assistants.

21. Is there a sign-in sheet for students who want to use the lab?

Sign-in sheets can be used for security reasons.

22. Is there information available in the lab to students who want to report malfunctioning equipment?

Students will use the lab equipment most frequently. If students are aware of the reporting process for malfunctioning equipment, delays in reporting and in repairing equipment can be minimized.

23. Are students responsible for providing their own videocassettes?

Requiring students to furnish their own tapes can be cost effective.

24. Are commercially produced videocassettes and CD-ROMs available for students to use in the lab?

There are a number of excellent commercially produced videocassettes and CD-ROMs for both lab and classroom use. For referrals on quality products contact the National Association of the Deaf.

Teachers' Performance Checklist

Teachers play an essential role in ensuring quality education. This performance evaluation not only assesses their performance but also the quality of the program as a whole. There is a misconception about the word *evaluation*. Professionals as well as non-professionals regard evaluation as a means of collecting information for disciplinary actions. That use of the word does not apply here. The main purpose of the following evaluation is not to prove, but to improve. A committed professional continuously monitors his or her performance to maintain his or her integrity. To maintain integrity, one would want to receive reviews from superiors and students who attend one's classes via the use of evaluation tools.

If the program does not have a means of collecting evaluative reviews from students, then it needs to develop an evaluation form for students to fill out. Appendix I can be used as a guide. If the program has already developed forms for students to evaluate their teachers, then answer the following questions. The questions here are listed in Appendix H.

1. Is the evaluation form students fill out at the end of a course a standard form used throughout the program?

Standardized student evaluations are one way of measuring the success of teachers and courses. It is imperative that the program provide a standard teacher/course evaluation form.

2. Does the evaluation form have space for the students to give open-ended comments about the teacher, the class, and/or the program?

The evaluation form should provide students the opportunity to evaluate the whole program and not just limit comments to the teacher or course work. There may be good teachers in a mediocre program. On the other hand, in an excellent program there may be some teachers who are not aware of their limitations.

3. Are the evaluation items on the form related to the teacher's performance in class?

See Appendix I for guidance. The items on the evaluation form must be specific to the teacher's classroom performance.

4. Are the evaluation items on the form also related to the course contents?

See Appendix I for guidance. Students should have the opportunity to review the course contents. This allows the program director/coordinator to determine whether the contents are appropriate for many skill levels.

5. Do teachers have the opportunity to review the evaluation forms after submitting final grades?

Students need to be assured that their grades will not be affected by what they write on their evaluation forms. The program director/ coordinator should set up procedures for collecting the forms at the end of the course, and the students should be assured of their confidentiality. Teachers can review the evaluation forms only after they submit final grades.

6. Are there written procedures in which the completed evaluation forms are submitted to a certain person?

Clearly written procedures in which students turn in the teacher/course evaluations to a designated person assure confidentiality for students who may want to write frank comments about their teachers.

7. Is there a person in the program who reviews the completed evaluation forms before teachers have access to them?

This review assures the credibility of the evaluation process.

8. In general, are there any assurances for students that there will be no reprisals from their teachers in the event s/he gives the teacher a poor evaluation rating?

Steps should be taken to minimize the chances that a student should suffer consequences for giving a teacher a poor evaluation rating. The evaluation form results can be tallied by a program secretary and reviewed by the director/coordinator before the teacher has access to the evaluations.

9. Are teachers given the opportunity to rebut in writing in the event they receive unsatisfactory evaluation ratings from their classes?

Teachers should be given the opportunity to defend themselves against cases where students with a grudge write an unfairly poor review of their teacher's performance.

10. Are the teachers' contract renewals contingent upon student evaluations, classroom observations by the program director/ coordinator, feedback from observers, and participation in staff meetings, etc.?

A careful gathering of documents to support a non-renewal of a contract or a termination of a teacher with low ratings is essential.

11. In the event a teacher continues to receive unsatisfactory evaluations from the students, is s/he subject to performance counseling, reprimand, probation, or termination?

Teachers should be given the right of due process when they receive unsatisfactory evaluations.

12. In the event a teacher continues to receive excellent evaluations, does s/he receive recognition?

Teachers need to be recognized for excellence. Letters of commendation, award plaques, and other forms of recognition can serve to boost teachers' motivation.

13. Does the evaluation reviewer write down additional comments on review forms for teachers to read?

The evaluation reviewer's comments can help teachers examine their strengths and weaknesses. If the assessment is without comment the teacher may wonder whether the evaluation forms were actually analyzed.

14. Are classroom observations conducted by the program director / coordinator?

Having the program director / coordinator observe the classroom can prove to be a valuable tool to assist teachers in finding ways to improve their teaching techniques. See Appendix J.

15. Does the program have a policy that allows teachers to attend conferences on Sign Language training and research, etc.?

Teachers attend conferences for the purpose of professional growth. Research on ASL is becoming available in greater quantity and detail, and teachers of ASL need to keep themselves abreast of what is happening in the field.

16. Does the program have a policy that requires teachers to attend in-service sessions?

In-service sessions provide essential information pertaining to policy changes, curriculum changes, etc., as well as announcements regarding upcoming conferences. The requirement of attending these sessions should be included in teachers' contracts.

17. Are in-service sessions held during non-class times?

Many colleges and universities employ full-time teachers who can benefit from in-services. Many other teachers are hired on a contract basis and do not have the same perks as a full-time teacher. These contract teachers should be able to attend in-service sessions also, even if they are offered outside of their teaching hours.

18. Do in-service trainings include, but not limit themselves to, the following?

A. Second language learning and acquisition?
B. Deaf culture?
C. Cross culture?
D. Media utilization?
E. Classroom management?
F. Approaches and methods of teaching?
G. Lesson planning?
H. How to handle problem students?
I. Evaluation methods?
J. Psychology of adult learners?
K. Ethics?

There are a number of topics that can be covered during in-service sessions. Because ASL is a distinctive language, in-services should be conducted in such a way as to raise the standards of teaching the language. Teachers need to be reminded constantly that teaching ASL is no trivial matter, as it may have been perceived in the early days of its teaching.

Environmental Aspects Checklist

The environmental aspects of a program play an important role, but often people take a classroom environment for granted. Necessities and possibilities for improvement are easily overlooked. For example, are classrooms appropriate for sign language instruction? Some classrooms have desks and chairs that can hamper the students from learning a visual–gestural language. What about lighting? Are the lights adequate for eyes to absorb the visual information that is being conveyed by the teacher and other students? If there were auditory noises outside of a French class, the teacher would probably go out and find a way to stop the noise. Is there such a thing as visual noise? Yes. For example, the flickering of a fluorescent light can be distracting not only to the students but also to the teacher.

This section examines items that pertain to the environmental aspects of a program's classrooms.

1. Does the program provide classrooms with adequate space?

An ideal classroom space for a class of no more than twelve students would be approximately thirty feet by thirty feet.* The Convention of Interpreter Trainers and ADFL recommend a maximum enrollment of twelve students (Cooper, 1997). The distance between the teacher and the center student's seat should be between twelve feet and fifteen feet. This space setup provides comfortable viewing distances so students can see the teacher without straining their eyes. See Figure 1.

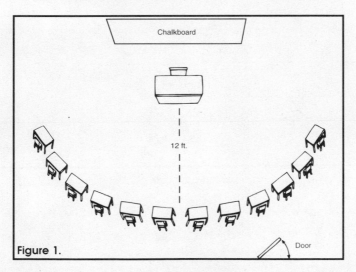

Chalkboard

12 ft.

Door

Figure 1.

---

*Mickey Fields, an architect employed by Gallaudet University specializing in designing buildings suitable for Deaf people, suggested this size.

2. Are the classrooms adequately lit (75–100 candlepower using the lumens meter for a sign language classroom)?

Ideal classroom lighting of 75–100 candlepower provides comfort to both the teacher and the students, and is valuable for comprehension purposes (Gayeski, 1995). A classroom with poor lighting would be like a classroom with poor acoustics that make it difficult for hearing students to hear each other.

3. If there is no fluorescent lighting in the classroom, then are the lights arranged so that they are approximately forty-five degrees in front of the teacher and in front of the students?

Lights that are arranged at forty-five degrees in front of the teacher and the students produce less shadows on people's faces. If the lights are placed directly above the teacher and/or the students, the lights produce dark shadows on people's faces that can interfere with understanding ASL. Another reason to have appropriate lighting is to reduce eye strain. See Figure 2.

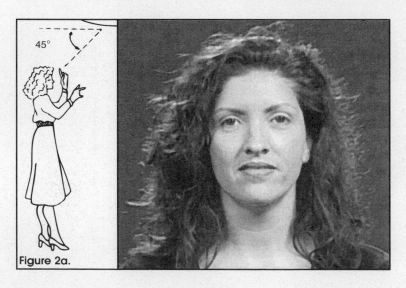

Figure 2a.

Figure 2b.

If the lights are behind the teacher and/or the students, this will create a silhouette effect. If the windows are behind the teacher and there are no window treatments, such as blinds, then the students will see a silhouette of the teacher. See Figure 3.

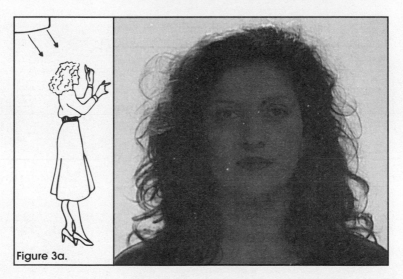

Figure 3a.

Figure 3b.

4. Are the seating arrangements made in such a way that all the students and the teacher can see each other easily?

The ideal seating arrangement is a semi-circle. This formation allows all students to see each other as well as the teacher. Because sign language is visual and gestural, it is essential for students to be able to see each other without difficulty. See Figure 4.

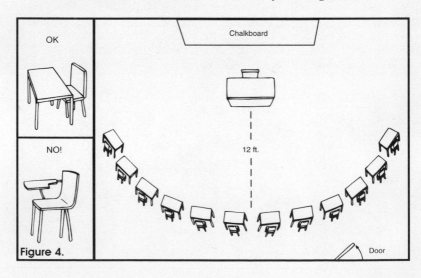

Figure 4.

42

5. Are the chairs in the classroom detached from the desks?

An ideal situation in a sign language class would be for the chairs to be separate from the desks. This allows students more freedom of movement. See Figure 4.

6. Is there a projection screen at the side of the classroom that is visible to all students?

The projection screen should be arranged so that all students can see it. The side placement of the screen allows the teacher to use the chalkboard without having to raise the screen and interrupt use of the overhead. See Figure 5.

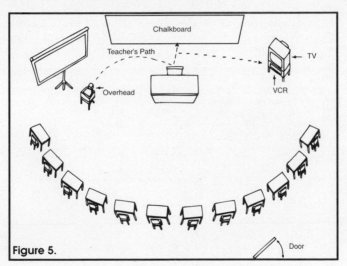

Chalkboard

Teacher's Path

TV

Overhead

VCR

Door

Figure 5.

7. Is the overhead projector or multimedia projector set on a cart low enough so that the projector is not blocking the students' view of the screen?

The cart that holds the projector tends to be high enough to accommodate the teacher. This is acceptable as long as the projector lens is not at the students' eye level, blocking their view. See Figure 5.

8. Is there a TV monitor with a VCR set at the other side of the classroom where it is visible to all students?

This arrangement allows the teacher to use the overhead/screen, the chalkboard, and the TV monitor with a VCR simultaneously without having to move equipment. NOTE: The TV screen should be at least thirty-five inches wide for optimal viewing. See Figure 5.

9. Is the seating arrangement such that students at either end of the semi-circle are within a forty-five degree angle to the screen, the chalkboard, and the TV monitor?

The students should be within a forty-five degree angle when viewing either the screen, the chalkboard, or the TV monitor. If a student is not within a forty-five degree angle, then viewing the media can be difficult because the image on the screen, the chalkboard, or the TV monitor becomes distorted. See Figure 6.

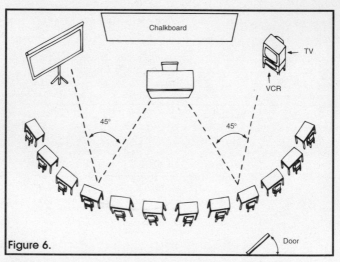

Figure 6.

10. Is the climate in the classroom comfortable?

This question refers to adequate ventilation, heating, and cooling.

11. Are the classrooms/buildings barrier-free for students with physical disabilities?

The Americans with Disabilities Act requires reasonable accommodations for those who are disabled. For more information contact:

Disability Rights Section
Civil Rights Division
US Department of Justice
P.O. Box 66738
Washington, DC 20035-6738

12. Is there a solid background in the front of the classroom with no clashing colors or loud designs that would interfere with the students' comprehension of their teacher's signing?

If there is a chalkboard in the front of the classroom, then there is no problem of visual noise. If there is no chalkboard, then the teacher must keep in mind that the background should be a solid color that contrasts with his or her skin color. Visually noisy backgrounds such as posters or pictures can be distracting.

13. Is the classroom prone to auditory noises?

It must be kept in mind that the vast majority of sign language students have normal hearing and are easily distracted by auditory noise.

14. Is there visual noise in the classroom or outside of the classroom?

A flickering fluorescent light is considered noisy for the eyes (Carver et al., 1991). If there is a window in a door at the front of the classroom, students can see the hallway traffic and become distracted. Teachers can also be distracted if a door with a window is in the back of the classroom. When there are visual distractions, and one person becomes distracted, then the entire class can become distracted.

15. Do teachers wear solid-colored shirts/blouses while teaching sign language? Is jewelry being worn?

Clothing that is not solid in color or jewelry that is flashy can be considered visual noise.

Supervisory Effectiveness Checklist

The spirit of this section is to assist the administrator in making sure that no part of a program is overlooked. Administrators can range from laissez-faire to dictatorial. The intent of this section is not to determine what type of an administrator a program has, but rather, how a program can be best served by its administrator. It is important to point out that some of the questions asked in this section may be deemed unnecessary for some programs if their program's administrators are familiar with the issues. These basic questions are geared for non-educational programs that may be found in churches, neighborhood classes, and the like.

1. Can you briefly and clearly state the program's philosophy toward teaching sign language?

There are no clear answers as to what is the right philosophical approach to teaching sign language. However, the philosophy reflects the program's belief in what should be taught in the classroom and how it should be taught. There are several questions a program director/coordinator should take into consideration. Should the use of voice in the classroom be permitted? Should fingerspelling be taught after the students attain a certain sign vocabulary, etc.?

2. Do you hold regular conferences with the teachers?

Regular conferences can occur as often as once a month or once every semester. It is at the administrator's discretion to decide the frequency of conferences with individual teachers or team members.

3. Are notes taken during staff meetings?

Minutes of the meetings can prevent misunderstandings between administrators and staff members.

4. Does the program have policies on substituting, disputes, submitting final grades, etc., with which both teachers and students need to comply?

Policies should cover substituting in case a teacher is not able to come to class. Also, what about making up classes that were canceled due to inclement weather? Is there a policy for handling a dispute between a teacher and a student over a final grade? There are other areas that need to be covered to protect the program's integrity. Policies are too often developed after problems arise.

5. Does the program have policies on registration deadlines, refunds, number of allowable absences for each class, etc., with which students must comply?

6. Do the teachers have any opportunity to assist the administrator in policy development?

If the teachers have some degree of ownership over policy development, they are more likely to support the program's policies.

7. In the case of terminating a teacher, does the program have a policy on due process?

A well-defined due process can minimize the chance of wrongful dismissal actions.

8. Does the program have a means of informing the public about its sign language classes?

There are several ways to advertise the program's class offerings, such as through local newspapers, newsletters, TV, radio, and the World Wide Web. The World Wide Web is an extremely effective means of letting the public know of the program. Setting up a home page on the Web is like telling the world that the programs exists.

9. Is the program director/coordinator readily available in any crisis?

There are some programs where the supervisor is not available to teachers and students. It is not mandatory for a supervisor to be present but teachers should know who to contact in case of an emergency.

10. Does the program have a system to keep teacher and student records?

Programs should have a place where student records can be kept under lock and key. Students may ask the program to send out documents verifying that they attended classes.

11. Does the program have access to information on how to deal with students with special needs?

The Americans with Disabilities Act mandates that all programs accommodate, within reason, students with special needs such as visual impairment, arthritis, cerebral palsy, etc.

12. Does the program allow some kind of direct involvement from the Deaf community such as an advisory committee, or a board of overseers that includes members of the Deaf community?

Getting the Deaf community involved in a program is very important. The Deaf community members can benefit a program a great deal as language models.

Budget Checklist

Many of the questions in this section may seem obvious to a seasoned administrator but are designed to benefit a new director/coordinator. To operate efficiently, a budget must be carefully considered. Expense projection must be maintained to account for emergencies. Expenses for equipment repairs or replacements cannot always be anticipated, but a program must be prepared for this type of expenditure.

1. Does the program have a line-item budget?

Item by item budgeting can facilitate some of the decision making required for a program. For example, revenue must be considered before salaries for teachers can be determined. Decisions about purchasing equipment need to be based on the budget. The following questions will assist in determining what items should be considered while preparing the budget.

2. Was a budget planned before the program was implemented?

Most programs will have predictable expenditures that can be calculated in advance of a program's implementation. After a program's implementation, the budget can be a used to see if the program is achieving the kinds of revenues predicted and incurring the expenses predicted.

3. Does the budget cover, but not limit itself to, expenses for the following?

A. Clerical support?

Clerical support is essential to running a successful program. A program director/coordinator can serve in the capacity of clerical staff when there are budgetary constraints. Clerical staff can handle registrations, record keeping, refunds, advertising, etc.

B. Announcements of class offerings?

A program needs to let the public know of its existence. Publicity can result in the generation of revenue. Advertisement in local newspapers, flyers, mass mailings, a World Wide Web home page, etc., should be taken into consideration.

C. Compensation for teachers?

The budgeted amount for compensating teachers must be taken into consideration above all the other budget items. Do not forget to pay taxes if the program is not affiliated with a non-profit organization.

D. Space rental (if applicable)?

There are sign language classes held at community centers, church basements, social agencies, etc., which may require rental funds.

E. Media equipment rental or purchasing?

Budget decisions to purchase or to rent visual-aid equipment such as VCRs, TV monitors, or overhead projectors, can be affected by in-coming revenue.

F. Insurance for missing or stolen equipment?

What happens if equipment is stolen and there is no budget for a replacement?

G. Videocassettes?

Students can be asked to purchase their own videocassettes. However, if the program expects teachers to prepare and use videocassettes, then a program's budget needs to include this expense.

H. Office supplies?

Letterhead, envelopes, paper clips, post-it notes, file folders, computers, printers, diskettes, and numerous other items can benefit a program.

I. Telephones, FAX, TTY?

Telephones, fax machines, and TTYs are needed to receive inquiries about the program.

J. Utilities?

Electricity, heat, and water bills need to be put in the budget if they are not included in the rent.

K. Professional development expenses?

Funds need to be considered to promote professional growth for teachers. Such expenses include travel expenses, per diem, and registration fees for attending conferences and workshops.

L. Traveling expenses for itinerant teachers?

Some programs make itinerant teachers available to teach in people's homes. Parents of a young deaf child can benefit a great deal if ASL training is done at home.

M. Postage?

Postage is needed to handle registration. Applicants send in their registration and fees to secure a place in class. Receipts need to be mailed back to the students, and this requires postage.

4. If the program charges tuition, does the program break even after paying expenses?

Breaking even is essential if the program does not receive subsidized funds. There are programs supported by a larger program, but other programs are self-supported, which requires breaking even. A pattern of breaking even can be maintained by establishing minimum enrollment for each class.

5. Does the program require minimal enrollment for a class to materialize?

A majority of programs have minimum enrollment requirements to determine whether a class should be held. Some programs require a minimum of eight to twelve students. There are other programs that require a minimum of twenty students, which is larger than the ideal size for a sign language class.

6. Does the program have a refund policy in case a student decides to withdraw from or drop a class?

Different programs have different policies for withdrawing from or dropping a class. Some programs will give full or partial refunds for withdrawing from a class during the first week. Some programs do not give any refunds if a student withdraws from a class after the first week. Programs should require a student to request a withdrawal or drop in writing.

Part Three

Appendices

Along with several other appendices, the eight areas covered in Part Two appear in this section. These eight evaluative lists have the following options:

S = Satisfactory. This would indicate that the question has been answered affirmatively and no changes are needed.

S/NI= Satisfactory/Needs Improvement. The program's current situation in regard to the question is acceptable, but some minor changes need to be made to improve the situation.

U = Unsatisfactory. The program's situation in regard to the question asked in not acceptable, but a corrective action can take place at an appropriate time.

U/NA = Unsatisfactory/Needs Attention. The program's situation in regard to the question asked in not satisfactory and is important enough to warrant immediate action to correct the situation.

S ☐   *S/NI* ☐   *U* ☐   *U/NA* ☐

Any appendices that do not follow this pattern will have explanations within that appendix.

Appendix A

Organizations and Addresses

Organizations

ASLTA
814 Thayer Avenue
Silver Spring, MD 20910

Gallaudet University
800 Florida Avenue
Washington DC 20002

National Association of the Deaf
814 Thayer Avenue
Silver Spring, MD 20910

National Technical Institute for the Deaf
52 Lomb Memorial Drive
Rochester, NY 14623

Publications

Chronicles of Higher Education
1255 23rd Street, NW
Washington DC 20037

Deaf Life
1095 Meigs Street
Rochester, NY 14620

Deaf Nation
1682 Bradford, NE
Grand Rapids, MI 49503

Journal of Deaf Studies
Center for Research Teaching and Learning
NTID
52 Lomb Memorial Drive
Rochester, NY 14623

Journal of Deaf Studies and Deaf Education
Oxford Press
20001 Evans Rd.
Cary, NC 27513

Sign Language Studies (Linstok Press)
4050 Blackburn Lane
Burtonsville, MD 20866

Silent News
133 Gaither Drive #E
Mount Laurel, NJ 08054

WWW Home Pages

Acceptance of ASL as Foreign Language by
Sherman Wilcox
http://www.unm.edu/~wilcox/ASLFL/as_fl.html

American Association of University Supervisors and
Coordinators of Foreign Language Programs
http://babel.uoregon.edu/romance/aausc/aausc.html

American Sign Language Teachers Association
http://www.isc.rit.edu/~ASLTAwww

Department of American Sign Language, Linguistics, and Interpretation at Gallaudet
http://www.gallaudet.edu/~aslweb/

Gallaudet University
http://www.gallaudet.edu/

National Technical Institute for the Deaf
http://www.isc.rit.edu.~418www/

Teachers of English to Speakers of Other Languages
http://www.tesol.edu/index.htm

Appendix B

Personnel Selection Checklist

1. Does the program advertise to recruit prospective ASL teachers in various publications such as Deaf Life, NAD Broadcaster, Deaf Nation, Sign Language Studies, Journal of Deaf Studies and Deaf Education, Deaf Studies, American Annals of the Deaf, Silent News, American Sign Language Teachers Association Newsletter, and Chronicles of Higher Education?

S ☐   S/NI ☐   U ☐   U/NA ☐

2. Does the program conduct national searches for prospective ASL teachers?

S ☐   S/NI ☐   U ☐   U/NA ☐

3. Does the program provide a clear and concise job description for the position being advertised?

S ☐   S/NI ☐   U ☐   U/NA ☐

4. Does the program require prospective ASL teachers to provide professional references if requested?

S ☐   S/NI ☐   U ☐   U/NA ☐

5. Is there a screening/interviewing committee in the program to review applications?

S ☐   S/NI ☐   U ☐   U/NA ☐

6. Does the screening/interviewing committee have established criteria for selecting prospective ASL teachers?

S ☐   S/NI ☐   U ☐   U/NA ☐

7. Do the criteria, mentioned in number 6, include, but not limit themselves to, the following?

A. Does the applicant have the required minimum number of years of experience teaching ASL?

S ☐   S/NI ☐   U ☐   U/NA ☐

B. Does the applicant hold the minimum degree requirement in his/her field or in related field(s)?

S ☐   S/NI ☐   U ☐   U/NA ☐

C. Does the applicant possess teaching credentials?

S ☐   S/NI ☐   U ☐   U/NA ☐

D. Does the applicant hold a certificate awarded by the American Sign Language Teachers Association (ASLTA) under the auspices of the National Association of the Deaf? If yes, which certificate— Provisional, Qualified or Professional?

S ☐   S/NI ☐   U ☐   U/NA ☐

E. Did the applicant attend various conferences and/or workshops pertaining to ASL teaching or any related fields?

S ☐   S/NI ☐   U ☐   U/NA ☐

F. Can the applicant use various types of media and technology for teaching ASL?

S ☐   S/NI ☐   U ☐   U/NA ☐

G. Is the applicant aware of the various approaches and methods of teaching a second language?

S ❑   *S/NI* ❑   *U* ❑   *U/NA* ❑

H. Does the applicant demonstrate tolerance for diversity among people, especially toward hearing people who want to learn ASL?

S ❑   *S/NI* ❑   *U* ❑   *U/NA* ❑

I. Is the applicant fluent in the use of American Sign Language?

S ❑   *S/NI* ❑   *U* ❑   *U/NA* ❑

J. Does the applicant show the ability to develop detailed lesson plans?

S ❑   *S/NI* ❑   *U* ❑   *U/NA* ❑

K. Does the applicant give a satisfactory answer on how a student with special learning needs is to be handled?

S ❑   *S/NI* ❑   *U* ❑   *U/NA* ❑

L. Does the applicant have training in developing relevant tests?

S ❑   *S/NI* ❑   *U* ❑   *U/NA* ❑

M. Is the applicant knowledgeable about the Acculturation Model related to successful second language acquisition?

S ❑   *S/NI* ❑   *U* ❑   *U/NA* ❑

N. Is the applicant knowledgeable about Deaf Culture?

S ❏   *S/NI* ❏   *U* ❏   *U/NA* ❏

O. Is the applicant capable of including cultural information in lesson plans?

S ❏   *S/NI* ❏   *U* ❏   *U/NA* ❏

8. Did the screening/interviewing committee develop a form detailing the criteria for selecting teachers to assist with the decision making process and selection of the final candidates for the job?

S ❏   *S/NI* ❏   *U* ❏   *U/NA* ❏

9. Did the interview committee develop a list of questions, organized so each member can take a turn asking questions of the applicant?

S ❏   *S/NI* ❏   *U* ❏   *U/NA* ❏

NOTES

Appendix C

Personnel Selection Form

Applicant:_____**Date Received:**_____

Requirements: **Check Yes or No**

Application received on or before the deadline   Yes ○   No ○
Resume/vita and Letter of Application   Yes ○   No ○
Language Proficiency Level—at least Advanced Plus (3+) Yes ○   No ○
Minimum three years of teaching ASL   Yes ○   No ○
Appropriate degree required for the job   Yes ○   No ○
Holder of an ASLTA certification   Yes ○   No ○
Letters of reference: #1   Yes ○   No ○
                        #2   Yes ○   No ○
                        #3   Yes ○   No ○

Rate as Poor, Fair, Good, or Excellent
(**P** = poor; **F** = fair; **G** = good; **E** = excellent)

A. Resume/Vita:	**P**	**F**	**G**	**E**
Quality of resume	○	○	○	○
Teaching experience	○	○	○	○
Affiliation with ASLTA	○	○	○	○
Participated in teacher training program	○	○	○	○
Attended ASL teachers workshops	○	○	○	○
Training in related field(s)	○	○	○	○

B. Letter of Application:				
Quality of the letter	○	○	○	○
Contents of the letter	○	○	○	○

	P	F	G	E
C. Letters of Reference:				
#1 Work History	O	O	O	O
Integrity	O	O	O	O
Comments by the writers	O	O	O	O
#2 Work History	O	O	O	O
Integrity	O	O	O	O
Comments by the writers	O	O	O	O
#3 Work History	O	O	O	O
Integrity	O	O	O	O
Comments by the writers	O	O	O	O
Interview:				
Appearance	O	O	O	O
Communication effectiveness	O	O	O	O
Schedule flexibility	O	O	O	O
Ability to be consistent in use of ASL	O	O	O	O

Appendix D

Interview Questions
(suggested questions)

1. Why do you want to teach ASL?

2. How long have you been teaching ASL?

3. Which level are you most comfortable teaching?

4. What books do you usually use to teach sign language?

5. What type of students have you worked with?
   (the answer will determine if the applicant is a good
   candidate for teaching a specific student, such as K–12, senior
   citizens, college students, etc.)

6. What training background do you have that would
   qualify you for the job?

7. What research or publications related to teaching sign
   language have you completed?

8. Do you have prepared lesson plans to show us? Can
   you explain them?

9. Do you have experience with the use of media
   equipment? If so, what?

10. Which days and hours are you available to teach? (This
    question is for applicants who are freelancing and have
    flexible hours.)

11. Are you usually available after class for students to ask questions or to have private conferences?

12. Do you have experience with students who have special needs? If so, what did you experience?

13. Suppose you have a student who is visually impaired and s/he wants to learn ASL. What would you do to accommodate that student?

14. What is your philosophy on teaching ASL without using voice? Explain your philosophy. (Generally voice is not used while teaching ASL.)

15. What do you know about Deaf Culture?

16. How do you present Deaf Culture information in your lesson plans?

17. Do you have any questions?

Appendix E

Curriculum Checklist

1. Was the curriculum developed through the efforts of content specialists along with a curriculum specialist?

S ☐   S/NI ☐   U ☐   U/NA ☐

2. Does the curriculum include the program's general goals related to student achievement levels?

S ☐   S/NI ☐   U ☐   U/NA ☐

3. Does the curriculum list specific performance objectives for each course?

S ☐   S/NI ☐   U ☐   U/NA ☐

4. Are behavioral terms used in the performance objectives?

S ☐   S/NI ☐   U ☐   U/NA ☐

5. Is the curriculum subject to periodic revisions?

S ☐   S/NI ☐   U ☐   U/NA ☐

6. Is flexibility allowed for last-minute changes in the curriculum if a teacher sees fit?

S ☐   S/NI ☐   U ☐   U/NA ☐

7. Is the teacher expected to inform others of any last-minute changes in the curriculum?

S ☐   S/NI ☐   U ☐   U/NA ☐

8. If a teacher does make changes to the curriculum and informs the director/coordinator, are other teachers informed of these changes in the curriculum?

S ☐   S/NI ☐   U ☐   U/NA ☐

9. Is the curriculum made readily available for teachers to review?

S ☐   S/NI ☐   U ☐   U/NA ☐

10. Is a word processor available for the staff members to write up or make changes in the curriculum?

S ☐   S/NI ☐   U ☐   U/NA ☐

11. Are syllabi distributed to the students on the first day of class?

S ☐   S/NI ☐   U ☐   U/NA ☐

12. Does the program have a means of evaluating its materials to determine their effectiveness?

S ☐   S/NI ☐   U ☐   U/NA ☐

13. Are the teaching materials subject to periodic change or replacement?

S ☐   S/NI ☐   U ☐   U/NA ☐

NOTES

Appendix F

Placement Interview Checklist

1. Does each course have a defined entrance level for determining a student's placement in the appropriate course and a defined exit level to ensure proper advancement to the next level course?

S ☐   S/NI ☐   U ☐   U/NA ☐

2. Are the exit level for the previous course and the entrance level for the next course consistent?

S ☐   S/NI ☐   U ☐   U/NA ☐

3. Are both the entrance and exit levels subject to periodic revisions?

S ☐   S/NI ☐   U ☐   U/NA ☐

4. Are students who have taken sign language classes elsewhere required to take placement interviews to determine appropriate placement?

S ☐   S/NI ☐   U ☐   U/NA ☐

5. If a student successfully attains the exit level for a course, is s/he automatically eligible for entry into the next level without undergoing a placement interview?

S ☐   S/NI ☐   U ☐   U/NA ☐

6. Are placement interviews scheduled regularly so prospective students can be interviewed prior to registration?

S ☐   *S/NI* ☐   *U* ☐   *U/NA* ☐

7. Are returning students required to have a placement interview after an absence of one year?

S ☐   *S/NI* ☐   *U* ☐   *U/NA* ☐

8. When conducting a placement interview, are the following factors taken into consideration?

   A. Prospective student's test anxiety?

S ☐   *S/NI* ☐   *U* ☐   *U/NA* ☐

   B. Interview room climate?

S ☐   *S/NI* ☐   *U* ☐   *U/NA* ☐

   C. Lighting quality in the interview room?

S ☐   *S/NI* ☐   *U* ☐   *U/NA* ☐

   D. Interviewer's qualities:

      Is s/he friendly?

S ☐   *S/NI* ☐   *U* ☐   *U/NA* ☐

      Is s/he compassionate?

S ☐   *S/NI* ☐   *U* ☐   *U/NA* ☐

      Does s/he possess excellent interpersonal skills?

S ☐   *S/NI* ☐   *U* ☐   *U/NA* ☐

Does s/he show consistency in placement
recommendations?

S ❑   *S/NI* ❑   *U* ❑   *U/NA* ❑

Does s/he know and understand the
contents of the program's curriculum?

S ❑   *S/NI* ❑   *U* ❑   *U/NA* ❑

Is s/he punctual in showing up for
the placement interviews?

S ❑   *S/NI* ❑   *U* ❑   *U/NA* ❑

Does s/he wear appropriate attire for the
interviews?

S ❑   *S/NI* ❑   *U* ❑   *U/NA* ❑

9. Are the results of the placement interviews made
available to the prospective students within a reasonable
amount of time?

S ❑   *S/NI* ❑   *U* ❑   *U/NA* ❑

NOTES

Appendix G

Media Utilization Checklist

1. Does the program have access to the following video equipment?

S ☐   S/NI ☐   U ☐   U/NA ☐

2. Does the program take security precautions in maintaining video equipment?

   A. Anchor pads?

   S ☐   S/NI ☐   U ☐   U/NA ☐

   B. Sign-up sheets for teachers who want to use the equipment?

   S ☐   S/NI ☐   U ☐   U/NA ☐

   C. A storage area with dead-bolt lock?

   S ☐   S/NI ☐   U ☐   U/NA ☐

   D. Security cables?

   S ☐   S/NI ☐   U ☐   U/NA ☐

   E. Identification marks on the equipment?

   S ☐   S/NI ☐   U ☐   U/NA ☐

F. Inventory information?

s ☐   s/NI ☐   u ☐   u/NA ☐

3. Does the program have VCR head cleaners?

s ☐   s/NI ☐   u ☐   u/NA ☐

4. Does the program provide teachers In-Service Training on media utilization?

s ☐   s/NI ☐   u ☐   u/NA ☐

5. If reservations for use of video equipment from a central facility on campus is required, do teachers know where to call or go to make reservations?

s ☐   s/NI ☐   u ☐   u/NA ☐

6. Do teachers know the policy for reserving and use of the video equipment?

s ☐   s/NI ☐   u ☐   u/NA ☐

7. Does the program use commercially produced videocassettes or CD-ROMs for use in the classroom and/or lab?

s ☐   s/NI ☐   u ☐   u/NA ☐

8. Does a program's teachers have the opportunity to produce their own video presentations for exclusive use in the classroom?

s ☐   s/NI ☐   u ☐   u/NA ☐

9. Does the program have an adequate number of blank videocassettes for teachers to use?

s ☐   s/NI ☐   u ☐   u/NA ☐

10. Are the program's videocassettes and CD-ROMs labeled and organized in such a way as to provide easy access?

s ❑   *S/NI* ❑   *u* ❑   *U/NA* ❑

11. Does the program provide various items that can be used for object manipulations in the classroom such as Lego toys, small dolls, etc.?

s ❑   *S/NI* ❑   *u* ❑   *U/NA* ❑

12.. Does the program provide teachers with funds to purchase teaching materials for their classes?

s ❑   *S/NI* ❑   *u* ❑   *U/NA* ❑

13. Do the teachers have access to the following items:

A. Overhead projector and a screen?

s ❑   *S/NI* ❑   *u* ❑   *U/NA* ❑

B. Blank transparencies?

s ❑   *S/NI* ❑   *u* ❑   *U/NA* ❑

C. Commercially prepared transparencies?

s ❑   *S/NI* ❑   *u* ❑   *U/NA* ❑

D. Slide projector and slide tray(s)?

s ❑   *S/NI* ❑   *u* ❑   *U/NA* ❑

E. Chalk or water-based markers?

s ❑   *S/NI* ❑   *u* ❑   *U/NA* ❑

F. Laptop computer and multimedia projector?

s ❑   *S/NI* ❑   *u* ❑   *U/NA* ❑

G. Copy machine?

S ☐   S/NI ☐   U ☐   U/NA ☐

14. Do the teachers have access to a word processor to type up lesson plans?

S ☐   S/NI ☐   U ☐   U/NA ☐

15. Does the program have a lab for students to use?

S ☐   S/NI ☐   U ☐   U/NA ☐

16. Does the program have a person (a student assistant) present at the lab to assist the students?

S ☐   S/NI ☐   U ☐   U/NA ☐

17. Is there adequate lighting in the lab for camcorders?

S ☐   S/NI ☐   U ☐   U/NA ☐

18. Does the lab have solid color backgrounds in front of which the student can stand while filming themselves with the camcorder?

S ☐   S/NI ☐   U ☐   U/NA ☐

19. Is the lab accessible to students during non-class times?

S ☐   S/NI ☐   U ☐   U/NA ☐

20. Are there procedures for both teachers and lab assistants to report malfunctioning visual media equipment?

S ☐   S/NI ☐   U ☐   U/NA ☐

21. Is there a sign-in sheet for students who want to use the lab?

S ☐   S/NI ☐   U ☐   U/NA ☐

22. Is there information available in the lab to students who want to report malfunctioning equipment?

S ☐   S/NI ☐   U ☐   U/NA ☐

23. Are students responsible for providing their own videocassettes?

S ☐   S/NI ☐   U ☐   U/NA ☐

24. Are commercially produced videocassettes and CD-ROMs available for students to use in the lab?

S ☐   S/NI ☐   U ☐   U/NA ☐

NOTES

Appendix H

Teachers' Performance Checklist

1. Is the evaluation form students fill out at the end of a course a standard form used throughout the program?

S ☐   S/NI ☐   U ☐   U/NA ☐

2. Does the evaluation form have space for the students to give open-ended comments about the teacher, the class, and/or the program?

S ☐   S/NI ☐   U ☐   U/NA ☐

3. Are the evaluation items on the form related to the teacher's performance in class?

S ☐   S/NI ☐   U ☐   U/NA ☐

4. Are the evaluation items on the form also related to the course contents?

S ☐   S/NI ☐   U ☐   U/NA ☐

5. Do teachers have the opportunity to review the evaluation forms after submitting final grades?

S ☐   S/NI ☐   U ☐   U/NA ☐

6. Are there written procedures in which the completed evaluation forms are submitted to a certain person?

S ☐   S/NI ☐   U ☐   U/NA ☐

7. Is there a person in the program who reviews the completed evaluation forms before teachers have access to them?

S ☐   S/NI ☐   U ☐   U/NA ☐

8. In general, are there any assurances for students that there will be no reprisals from their teachers in the event s/he gives the teacher a poor evaluation rating?

S ☐   S/NI ☐   U ☐   U/NA ☐

9. Are teachers given the opportunity to rebut in writing in the event they receive unsatisfactory evaluation ratings from their classes?

S ☐   S/NI ☐   U ☐   U/NA ☐

10. Are the teachers contract renewals contingent upon student evaluations, classroom observations by the program director/coordinator, feedback from observers, and participation in staff meetings, etc.?

S ☐   S/NI ☐   U ☐   U/NA ☐

11. In the event a teacher continues to receive unsatisfactory evaluations from the students, is s/he subject to performance counseling, reprimand, probation, or termination?

S ☐   S/NI ☐   U ☐   U/NA ☐

12. In the event a teacher continues to receive excellent evaluations, does s/he receive recognition?

S ☐   S/NI ☐   U ☐   U/NA ☐

13. Does the evaluation reviewer write down additional comments on review forms for teachers to read?

S ❑   *S/NI* ❑   *U* ❑   *U/NA* ❑

14. Are classroom observations conducted by the program director/coordinator?

S ❑   *S/NI* ❑   *U* ❑   *U/NA* ❑

15. Does the program have a policy that allows teachers to attend conferences on Sign Language training and research, etc.?

S ❑   *S/NI* ❑   *U* ❑   *U/NA* ❑

16. Does the program have a policy that requires teachers to attend in-service sessions?

S ❑   *S/NI* ❑   *U* ❑   *U/NA* ❑

17. Are In-Service sessions held during non-class times?

S ❑   *S/NI* ❑   *U* ❑   *U/NA* ❑

18. Do in-service trainings include, but not limit themselves to, the following?

A. Second language learning and acquisition?

S ❑   *S/NI* ❑   *U* ❑   *U/NA* ❑

B. Deaf Culture?

S ❑   *S/NI* ❑   *U* ❑   *U/NA* ❑

C. Cross culture?

S ❑   *S/NI* ❑   *U* ❑   *U/NA* ❑

D. Media utilization?

S ☐   S/NI ☐   U ☐   U/NA ☐

E. Classroom management?

S ☐   S/NI ☐   U ☐   U/NA ☐

F. Approaches and methods of teaching?

S ☐   S/NI ☐   U ☐   U/NA ☐

G. Lesson planning?

S ☐   S/NI ☐   U ☐   U/NA ☐

H. How to handle problem students?

S ☐   S/NI ☐   U ☐   U/NA ☐

I. Evaluation methods?

S ☐   S/NI ☐   U ☐   U/NA ☐

J. Psychology of adult learners?

S ☐   S/NI ☐   U ☐   U/NA ☐

K. Ethics?

S ☐   S/NI ☐   U ☐   U/NA ☐

NOTES

Appendix I

Student Evaluation on
Course and Instructor *(use as a guideline)*

STUDENT EVALUATION OF COURSE

Name of instructor teaching course:_____

Department:_____ **Date of evaluation:**_____

Department course code/number/section number:_____

Indicate how much you agree or disagree with each of the statements in sections I, II, and III.
(**SD** = strongly disagree; **D** = disagree; **A** = agree; **SA** = strongly agree)

I. THE CLASS	SD	D	A	SA
1. Course policies and requirements were clearly explained at the beginning of the semester.	O	O	O	O
2. This course stimulated my thinking.	O	O	O	O
3. The textbooks and handouts were good.	O	O	O	O
4. The grading system was fair.	O	O	O	O
5. A fair amount of work was assigned.	O	O	O	O
6. The homework assignments were just challenging enough.	O	O	O	O
7. The tests were just challenging enough.	O	O	O	O
8. The class was interesting.	O	O	O	O

II. THE INSTRUCTOR

	SD	D	A	SA
1. The instructor used visual aids (projector, slides, chalkboard, etc.) very well.	O	O	O	O
2. The instructor was well prepared for class.	O	O	O	O.

3. The instructor's lectures and explanations were clear ○ ○ ○ ○

4. The instructor was enthusiastic about teaching this class. ○ ○ ○ ○

5. The instructor was able to answer questions. ○ ○ ○ ○

6. The instructor was able to include Deaf Culture information in lesson presentations. ○ ○ ○ ○

III. STUDENT–TEACHER INTERACTION

	SD	D	A	SA
1. The instructor encouraged discussion and questions.	○	○	○	○
2. The instructor was available during office hours.	○	○	○	○
3. The instructor was willing to meet with me individually if I needed help.	○	○	○	○
4. The instructor maintained eye contact with all the members of the class.	○	○	○	○

IV. GENERAL QUESTIONS

1. I was required to take this course. Yes ○   No ○

2. This course is a prerequisite to another one I want to take. Yes ○   No ○

3. I am majoring or in a degree program in the department offering this course. Yes ○   No ○

4. I am considering selecting the department as my major. Yes ○   No ○

5. Overall, I rate this instructor: Poor ○   Fair ○   Good ○   Excellent ○

6. Overall, I rate this course: Poor ○   Fair ○   Good ○   Excellent ○

COMMENTS:

_____

_____

_____

Source: Dept. of American Sign Language, Linguistics, and Interpretation, Gallaudet University, Washington, DC.

Appendix J

Observation Sheet

REPORT OF CLASS OBSERVATION

Background Information

A. Name of faculty member: _____

B. Name of evaluator:_____

C. Date of evaluation:_____ Class size _____

D. Course name:_____
   Course no. and section: _____

E. Length of class *(in minutes)*:_____
   Length of observation *(in minutes)*:_____

ASSESSMENT

Rate each area on a scale from 1 (strongly disagree) to 5 (strongly agree).

1 ——————— 2 ——————— 3 ——————— 4 ——————— 5
strongly disagree   strongly agree

Part A: The Lesson

_____ 1. Objectives for the day were made clear.

_____ 2. Class time was well utilized; time allotted was appropriate for
           the material covered.

_____ 3. Material was presented clearly and in a way comprehensible to
           the students.

_____ 4. Goals for the day were fully achieved.

_____ 5. The pace of class was appropriate.

_____ 6. Other:_____

Explain your ratings:_____

_____

_____

_____

Rate each area on a scale from 1 (strongly disagree) to 5 (strongly agree).

1 ——————— 2 ——————— 3 ——————— 4 ——————— 5
strongly disagree   strongly agree

Part B: The Instructor *(Continue using the 5-point rating scale.)*

_____ 1. The instructor was knowledgeable about the material covered.

_____ 2. The instructor was well prepared for class.

_____ 3. The instructor was enthusiastic about the subject matter and enjoyed sharing knowledge with the students.

_____ 4. The instructor related to the students in a positive way.

_____ 5. Visual media were used effectively, if employed.

_____ 6. Other:_____

Explain your ratings:_____

_____

_____

_____

Part C: Student–Teacher Interaction *(Continue using the 5-point rating scale.)*

_____ 1. The instructor used a mode of instruction appropriate for the students and the material.

_____ 2. Student participation was encouraged where appropriate.

_____ 3. Students and the instructor were able to communicate easily and clearly with each other.

_____ 4. The classroom was effectively managed; the class was properly facilitated.

_____ 5. The instructor was able to accommodate different learning styles, if necessary.

_____ 6. The students appeared interested and attentive.

_____ 7. The instructor fielded questions appropriately.

_____ 8. Other: _____

Explain your ratings:_____

_____

_____

_____

Part D: Summary of Instructor's Greatest Strengths:

_____

_____

_____

_____

_____

Part E: Summary of Areas Needing Improvement and Suggestions for Further Professional Development:

_____

_____

_____

_____

_____

Overall Rating
(circle)

Lowest   Highest

1   2   3   4   5

Signature:_____Date_____

(Person completing evaluation)

Appendix K

Environmental Aspects Checklist

1. Does the program provide classrooms with adequate space?

S ☐   S/NI ☐   U ☐   U/NA ☐

2. Are the classrooms adequately lit (75 - 100 candlepower using the lumens meter for a sign language classroom)?

S ☐   S/NI ☐   U ☐   U/NA ☐

3. If there is no fluorescent lighting in the classroom, then are the lights arranged so that they are approximately 45 degrees in front of the teacher and in front of the students?

S ☐   S/NI ☐   U ☐   U/NA ☐

4. Are the seating arrangements made in such a way that all the students and the teacher can see each other easily?

S ☐   S/NI ☐   U ☐   U/NA ☐

5. Are the chairs in the classroom detached from the desks?

S ☐   S/NI ☐   U ☐   U/NA ☐

6. Is there a projection screen at the side of the classroom that is visible to all students?

S ☐   S/NI ☐   U ☐   U/NA ☐

7. Is the overhead projector or multimedia projector set on a cart low enough so that the projector is not blocking the students' view of the screen?

    S ❏   *S/NI* ❏   *U* ❏   *U/NA* ❏

8. Is there a TV monitor with a VCR set at the other side of the classroom where it is visible to all students?

    S ❏   *S/NI* ❏   *U* ❏   *U/NA* ❏

9. Is the seating arrangement such that students at either end of the semi-circle are within a 45 degree angle to the screen, the chalkboard, and the TV monitor?

    S ❏   *S/NI* ❏   *U* ❏   *U/NA* ❏

10. Is the climate in the classroom comfortable?

    S ❏   *S/NI* ❏   *U* ❏   *U/NA* ❏

11. Are the classrooms/buildings barrier-free for students with physical disabilities?

    S ❏   *S/NI* ❏   *U* ❏   *U/NA* ❏

12. Is there a solid background in the front of the classroom with no clashing colors or loud designs that would interfere with the students' comprehension of their teacher's signing?

    S ❏   *S/NI* ❏   *U* ❏   *U/NA* ❏

13. Is the classroom prone to auditory noises?

    S ❏   *S/NI* ❏   *U* ❏   *U/NA* ❏

14. Is there visual noise in the classroom or outside of the classroom?

S ☐   S/NI ☐   U ☐   U/NA ☐

15. Do teachers wear solid-colored shirts/blouses while teaching sign language? Is jewelry being worn?

S ☐   S/NI ☐   U ☐   U/NA ☐

NOTES

Appendix L
Supervisory Effectiveness Checklist

✅

1. Can you briefly and clearly state the program's philosophy toward teaching sign language?

    S ☐   *S/NI* ☐   *U* ☐   *U/NA* ☐

2. Do you hold regular conferences with the teachers?

    S ☐   *S/NI* ☐   *U* ☐   *U/NA* ☐

3. Are notes taken during staff meetings?

    S ☐   *S/NI* ☐   *U* ☐   *U/NA* ☐

4. Does the program have policies on substituting, disputes, submitting final grades, etc., with which both teachers and students need to comply?

    S ☐   *S/NI* ☐   *U* ☐   *U/NA* ☐

5. Does the program have policies on registration deadlines, refunds, number of allowable absences for each class, etc., with which students must comply?

    S ☐   *S/NI* ☐   *U* ☐   *U/NA* ☐

6. Do the teachers have any opportunity to assist the administrator in policy development?

    S ☐   *S/NI* ☐   *U* ☐   *U/NA* ☐

7. In the case of terminating a teacher, does the program have a policy on due process?

S ☐   S/NI ☐   U ☐   U/NA ☐

8. Does the program have a means of informing the public about its sign language classes?

S ☐   S/NI ☐   U ☐   U/NA ☐

9. Is the program director/coordinator readily available in any crisis?

S ☐   S/NI ☐   U ☐   U/NA ☐

10. Does the program have a system to keep teacher and student records?

S ☐   S/NI ☐   U ☐   U/NA ☐

11. Does the program have access to information on how to deal with students with special needs?

S ☐   S/NI ☐   U ☐   U/NA ☐

12. Does the program allow some kind of direct involvement from the Deaf community such as an advisory committee, or a board of overseers that includes members of the Deaf community?

S ☐   S/NI ☐   U ☐   U/NA ☐

NOTES

Appendix M
Budget Checklist

1. Does the program have a line-item budget?

     S ☐   *S/NI* ☐   *U* ☐   *U/NA* ☐

2. Was a budget planned before the program was implemented?

     S ☐   *S/NI* ☐   *U* ☐   *U/NA* ☐

3. Does the budget cover, but not limit itself to, expenses for the following?

     A. Clerical support?

     S ☐   *S/NI* ☐   *U* ☐   *U/NA* ☐

     B. Announcements of class offerings?

     S ☐   *S/NI* ☐   *U* ☐   *U/NA* ☐

     C. Compensation for teachers?

     S ☐   *S/NI* ☐   *U* ☐   *U/NA* ☐

     D. Space rental (if applicable)?

     S ☐   *S/NI* ☐   *U* ☐   *U/NA* ☐

     E. Media equipment rental or purchasing?

     S ☐   *S/NI* ☐   *U* ☐   *U/NA* ☐

F. Insurance for missing or stolen equipment?

S ❏   *S/NI* ❏   *U* ❏   *U/NA* ❏

G. Videocassettes?

S ❏   *S/NI* ❏   *U* ❏   *U/NA* ❏

H. Office supplies?

S ❏   *S/NI* ❏   *U* ❏   *U/NA* ❏

I. Telephones, FAX, TTY?

S ❏   *S/NI* ❏   *U* ❏   *U/NA* ❏

J. Utilities?

S ❏   *S/NI* ❏   *U* ❏   *U/NA* ❏

K. Professional development expenses?

S ❏   *S/NI* ❏   *U* ❏   *U/NA* ❏

L. Traveling expenses for itinerant teachers?

S ❏   *S/NI* ❏   *U* ❏   *U/NA* ❏

M. Postage?

S ❏   *S/NI* ❏   *U* ❏   *U/NA* ❏

4. If the program charges tuition, does the program break even after paying expenses?

S ❏   *S/NI* ❏   *U* ❏   *U/NA* ❏

5. Does the program require minimal enrollment for a class to materialize?

S ❏   *S/NI* ❏   *U* ❏   *U/NA* ❏

6. Does the program have a refund policy in case a student decides to withdraw from or drop a class?

S ☐ S/NI ☐ U ☐ U/NA ☐

NOTES

Bibliography

Alderson, C., & Beratta, A. (Eds.). *Evaluating second language education*. Cambridge, MA: Cambridge University Press.

Aleomoni, L. M. (1972). *Illinois course evaluation questionnaire* (CEO) results interpretation manual form 66 and form 32. (Research Report No. 331) Urbana University of Illinois. Measurement and Research Division, Office of Instructional Resource.

Baker, C., & Cokely, D. (1980). *American Sign Language: A teacher's text on curriculum, method, and evaluation*. Washington, DC: Gallaudet Press.

Callahan, J. F., & Clark, L. H. (1982). *Teaching in the middle and secondary schools*. (2nd edition). New York: Macmillan Publishing Co., Inc.

Carver, S., Doull, E., Read, D., Batal, J., and Bertin, V. (1991). *Environmental factors in the education of the deaf*. Ottawa: Canada Association of the Deaf.

Cokely, D. (1986, Spring). College level sign language programs: A resource list. William Stokoe (Ed.), Sign Language Studies. Silver Spring, MD: Linstok Press, Inc.

Cooper, S. (1997). Academic status of sign language programs in institutions of higher education in the USA. (Unpublished doctoral dissertation: Gallaudet University).

Fitz-Gibbon, C.T., & Morris, L. L. (1987). *How to design a program evaluation*. Newbury Park, CA: Sage Publications.

Gayeski, D. (1995). *Designing communication and learning environment*. Englewoods, NJ: Educational Technical Publications.

Bibliography

Gingras, R. (1981). *Second language acquisition & foreign language teaching*. Arlington, VA: Center for Applied Linguistics.

Isaac, S. & Michael, W. B. (1983). *Handbook in research and evaluation*. (2nd edition.). San Diego: Edits Publishers.

Jacobs, R. (1996) "Just How Hard Is It to Learn ASL! The Case for ASL as a Truly Foreign Language". In C. Lucas (Ed.). *Sociolinguistics in deaf community series, multicultural aspects of sociolinguistics in deaf communities*. Washington, DC: Gallaudet University Press.

Kemp, M. (1988). Self-assessment of a sign language program. *American annals of the deaf*. **133,** p. 349-55.

Kemp, M. (In press). An acculturation model for learners of American Sign Language. In C. Lucas (Ed.). *Sociolinguistics in deaf community series, pinky extension and eye gaze: Language use in deaf communities*. Washington, DC: Gallaudet University Press.

Kepner, C. H., & Tregae, B. B. (1981). *The new rational manager*. Princeton, NJ: Princeton Research Press

Lynch, B. (1996). *Language program evaluation: Theory and practice*. Cambridge, MA: Cambridge University Press.

Mager, J. (1984). *Measuring instructional results or got a match?* (2nd edition.). Balmont, CA: Lake Publishing Co.

Mager, J. (1984). *Preparing instructional objectives* (2nd edition.). Balmont, CA: Lake Publishing Co.

McIntire, M. L. (1981). Evaluating sign language teaching and learning materials. In F. Caccamise, M. Garretson, & U. Bellugi (Eds.). *Teaching sign language as a second/foreign language*. Silver Spring, MD: National Association of the Deaf, p. 194.

Morris, L. L., & Fitz-Gibbon, C. T. (1978). Evaluator's handbook. In L. L. Morris (Ed.). *Program evaluation kit*. Newbury Park, CA: Sage Publications.

Bibliography

Popham, J. W. (1975). *Educational evaluation*. Englewood Cliffs, NJ: Prentice-Hall, Inc.

Sanders, J. R., (1992). *Evaluating school programs: an educator's guide*. The Program Evaluation Guides for Schools. Richard M. Jaeger (Series Ed.) Newbury Park, CA: Corwin Press, Inc.

Schaffarzick, J., Sykes, G. (Eds.). (1979). *Value conflicts and curriculum issues*. Berkeley, CA: McCutchan Publishing Corp.

Stufflebeam, D., Foley, W. J., Gephart, W. J., Guba, E. C., Hamond, R. L., Merriman, H. O., & Provus, M. M. (1971). *Educational evaluation and decision making*. Itasca, ILL: F. E. Peacock.

Tuckman, B. W. (1979). *Evaluating Instructional Programs*. Boston: Allyn and Bacon, Inc.

Tyler, R. (1942). General Statement on evaluation. *Journal of Educational Research*, **35**, 92-50L.

Windham, D., & Chapman, D. (1990). *The evaluation of educational efficiency: Constraints, issues and policies*. Greenwich, CT: JAI Press, Inc.

Reader Survey

Thank you for taking the time to read this book. I would appreciate if I could ask for a bit more of your time. The following survey is meant to collect information about existing sign language programs. Data collected in responses will be analyzed for use in a possible second edition of this book. On your own paper, please respond to the following questions , making sure to number your answers to correspond with the question numbers, and mail your response to DawnSignPress, 6130 Nancy Ridge Drive, San Diego, CA 92121, or you can fill out the survey at our web site at www.dawnsign.com under *For Teachers Only*. Your input is very valuable and will help contribute to the future of sign language evaluation.

Name:_____

School or Department where you work:_____

Address:_____

City:_____

State:_____Zip:_____

Phone Number (voice/tty):_____

E-mail:_____

1. What is your position in the program?

2. What degree(s) do you hold?

3. How many years have you been in the field of ASL teaching?

4. What is the type of program with which you are affiliated (college/university, community college, secondary school, elementary school, social agency, church program)?

5. What specific department in your organization, if any, does your program operate under?

6. How many years has your program been in existence?

7. How many ASL classes does your program offer?

ASL I   _____

ASL II   _____

ASL III   _____

ASL IV   _____

ASL V   _____

ASL VI   _____

Other   _____

8. What is the minimum enrollment required for a class to be held?

9. What is the maximum class size allowed?

10. Do you have a waiting list for students who want to take a class in the event that space becomes available?

11. What textbooks do you use for each class level?

ASL I   _____

ASL II   _____

ASL III   _____

ASL IV   _____

ASL V   _____

ASL VI   _____

Other   _____

12. In the Personnel Selection Checklist on page 8 criteria for selecting ASL teachers is listed. Which of these criteria does your program use to determine the applicant's qualifications?

13. What additional criteria does your program consider?

14. The Personnel Selection Form on page 12 lists items that help determine an applicant's qualifications. Which of these items does your program use to help evaluate applicant qualifications?

15. What additional items does your program use?

16. The Curriculum Checklist on page 17 lists items related to the quality of the program's curriculum. Which of the items does your program use?

17. Which additional items does your program use?

18. The Placement Interview Checklist on page 23 lists the items that should be taken into consideration for doing interviews. Which of these items does your program use?

19. What other interview questions do you ask? Why do you ask these questions?

20. The Media Utilization Checklist on page 27 lists the equipment needed for ASL instruction as well as precautions to assure security. What listed equipment does your program use?

21. What additional equipment does your program use?

22. What security measures does your program use for equipment?

23. The Teachers' Performance Checklist on page 33 lists the procedures for collecting data from the students as well as for the assurance of due process for teachers whose skills are being questioned. Are the procedures listed standard in your program?

24. If not, what does your program do to collect evaluations from students?

25. What kind of due process does your program have for teachers whose skills are being questioned?

26. The Student Evaluation Form on Course and Instructor on page 000 was included as a guideline. Which questions does your program use?

27. If none, what alternate questions does your program use in its evaluation forms?

28. The Environmental Aspects Checklist on page 38 lists factors related to the classroom and the lab. Which of the listed factors does your program consider when selecting a classroom or designing a lab?

29. What other factors does your program take into consideration when selecting a classroom or designing a lab?

30. The Supervisory Effectiveness Checklist on page 46 lists the items that determine the effectiveness of the program director/coordinator. Which items does your program use?

31. What other items does your program use to determine the director/coordinator's effectiveness?

32. The Budget Checklist on page 49 lists expense items needed to operate a program. Which items does your program use to prepare a budget?

33. What other expense items does your program take into consideration for budget preparation?